It's

only

one

semester

The
D.I.Y.
Student Planner

by
Joy L. Kieffer

It's only one semester: 6 Month College/High School Student Planner. Prioritize classes and activities. Undated calendars, blank lists, graphs, schedule. Class pages-projects, labs, exams, contacts.

Published by Hidden Cache Media
Copyright 2017 Joy L. Kieffer, Wallingford, PA
Artwork and cover design by Joy L. Kieffer
Author photos by HR Kelley

ISBN-13: 978-0-9981078-1-3
ISBN-10: 0-9981078-1-6

Available from Amazon.com, and other retail outlets.
Available in bulk quantities. Visit www.joykieffer.com to learn more about how you can use this and other planners to raise funds for your group or cause. These planners help us in our work to feed students through The Giving Garden food pantry, just one aspect of Lifewerks, Inc. To learn more, go to lifewerks.org.

"As a person who has a strong bent towards creativity and spontaneity, but also one who knows they need a planner to "get stuff done" and be productive, I love the layout and content of the Student Planner. For me it has just enough structure to help me be more intentional. But it also has enough "free space" for me to be creative as I brainstorm and dream. I can draw my thoughts out or write them out, whatever works best for me at any given moment."

Jerome Stockert
Campus Minister
Arkansas State University
Baptist Collegiate Ministry

"Finally, a planner tailored for a college student's semester. Too often, college students only use a portion of a planner. This planner is for a semester and offers the student several options, including a weekly overview, daily plans, weekly plans, and monthly plans. Furthermore, it leaves room for the creative mind to plan in an out-of-the box way. The proceeds are to provide for Joy's food ministry."

Dr. Michael Brennan
Liberty University professor
School of Music

Dedication

To our volunteers, who make Lifewerks and the The Giving Garden possible. Your dedication and enthusiasm are inspiring! I have the best volunteers in the world! Sorry, rest of the world, you'll have to find your own!

Instructions

Oh, wait, you're a rebel and creative person! You don't need instructions. So, use this planner however you want.

There are no dates filled in; there are no suggestions for what to put in what box (other than the form for your individual classes.) Since you might possibly want to pass those classes, it might be a good idea to fill in the requirements. No pressure. It's your life.

Sadly, I simply couldn't get around the fact that there are seven days in a week, and they all have names. But you can rename them if you want.

Class Schedule

Time	Monday	Tuesday	Wednesday	Thursday

Friday	Saturday	Sunday	

Class

Office Hours	Code

Instructor

Email	Phone	Room #

Assistant

Email	Phone	

Late	Absent	Office Location

Lab Dates

Projects

Start Date	Due Date	Project

Exams

Date	Location	Notes/Info

Class

Office Hours	Code

Instructor

Email	Phone	Room #

Assistant

Email	Phone	

Late	Absent	Office Location

Lab Dates

Projects

Start Date	Due Date	Project

Exams

Date	Location	Notes/Info

Class

Office Hours	Code

Instructor

Email	Phone	Room #

Assistant

Email	Phone	

Late	Absent	Office Location

Lab Dates

Projects

Start Date	Due Date	Project

Exams

Date	Location	Notes/Info

Class

Office Hours	Code

Instructor

Email	Phone	Room #

Assistant

Email	Phone	

Late	Absent	Office Location

Lab Dates

Projects

Start Date	Due Date	Project

Exams

Date	Location	Notes/Info

Class

	Office Hours	Code

Instructor

Email	Phone	Room #

Assistant

Email	Phone	

Late	Absent	Office Location

Lab Dates

Projects

Start Date	Due Date	Project

Exams

Date	Location	Notes/Info

Class	Office Hours	Code

Instructor

Email	Phone	Room #

Assistant

Email	Phone	

Late	Absent	Office Location

Lab Dates

Projects

Start Date	Due Date	Project

Exams

Date	Location	Notes/Info

Class

Class	Office Hours	Code

Instructor

Email	Phone	Room #

Assistant

Email	Phone	

Late	Absent	Office Location

Lab Dates

Projects

Start Date	Due Date	Project

Exams

Date	Location	Notes/Info

Class

Office Hours	Code

Instructor

Email	Phone	Room #

Assistant

Email	Phone	

Late	Absent	Office Location

Lab Dates

Projects

Start Date	Due Date	Project

Exams

Date	Location	Notes/Info

Class

Office Hours	Code

Instructor

Email	Phone	Room #

Assistant

Email	Phone	

Late	Absent	Office Location

Lab Dates

Projects

Start Date	Due Date	Project

Exams

Date	Location	Notes/Info

Class

Office Hours	Code

Instructor

Email	Phone	Room #

Assistant

Email	Phone	

Late	Absent	Office Location

Lab Dates

Projects

Start Date	Due Date	Project

Exams

Date	Location	Notes/Info

Class

Office Hours	Code

Instructor

Email	Phone	Room #

Assistant

Email	Phone

Late	Absent	Office Location

Lab Dates

Projects

Start Date	Due Date	Project

Exams

Date	Location	Notes/Info

Monday	Tuesday	Wednesday	Thursday

Friday	Saturday	Sunday	

Monday	Tuesday	Wednesday	Thursday

Friday	Saturday	Sunday	

Monday	Tuesday	Wednesday	Thursday

Friday	Saturday	Sunday	

Monday	Tuesday	Wednesday	Thursday

Friday	Saturday	Sunday	

Monday	Tuesday	Wednesday	Thursday

Friday	Saturday	Sunday	

Monday	Tuesday	Wednesday	Thursday

Friday	Saturday	Sunday	

Monday		
Tuesday		
Wednesday		

Thursday		
Friday		
Saturday		Sunday	

Monday		
Tuesday		
Wednesday		

Thursday

Friday

Saturday

Sunday

Monday		
Tuesday		
Wednesday		

Thursday

Friday

Saturday

Sunday

Monday		
Tuesday		
Wednesday		

Thursday

Friday

Saturday

Sunday

Monday		
Tuesday		
Wednesday		

Thursday

Friday

Saturday

Sunday

Monday		
Tuesday		
Wednesday		

Thursday	
Friday	
Saturday	**Sunday**

Monday

Tuesday

Wednesday

Thursday

Friday

Saturday

Sunday

Monday

Tuesday

Wednesday

Thursday

Friday

Saturday

Sunday

Monday			
Tuesday			
Wednesday			

Thursday

Friday

Saturday

Sunday

Monday		
Tuesday		
Wednesday		

Thursday

Friday

Saturday

Sunday

Monday		
Tuesday		
Wednesday		

Thursday

Friday

Saturday

Sunday

Monday

Tuesday

Wednesday

Thursday

Friday

Saturday

Sunday

Monday			
Tuesday			
Wednesday			

Thursday

Friday

Saturday

Sunday

Monday		
Tuesday		
Wednesday		

Thursday	
Friday	
Saturday	Sunday

Monday		
Tuesday		
Wednesday		

Thursday

Friday

Saturday

Sunday

Monday		
Tuesday		
Wednesday		

Thursday

Friday

Saturday

Sunday

Monday		
Tuesday		
Wednesday		

Thursday

Friday

Saturday

Sunday

Monday

Tuesday

Wednesday

Thursday

Friday

Saturday		**Sunday**	

Monday

Tuesday

Wednesday

Monday		
Tuesday		
Wednesday		

Thursday	
Friday	
Saturday	**Sunday**

Monday		
Tuesday		
Wednesday		

Thursday

Friday

Saturday

Sunday

Monday		
Tuesday		
Wednesday		

Thursday

Friday

Saturday

Sunday

Monday		
Tuesday		
Wednesday		

Thursday

Friday

Saturday

Sunday

Monday			
Tuesday			
Wednesday			

Thursday

Friday

Saturday

Sunday

Monday

Tuesday

Wednesday

Thursday	
Friday	
Saturday	**Sunday**

Monday		
Tuesday		
Wednesday		

Thursday

Friday

Saturday

Sunday

Monday		
Tuesday		
Wednesday		

Thursday

Friday

Saturday

Sunday

About the Author

Joy has long been frustrated with student planners that don't take into consideration the simple fact that classes change from one semester to the next.

She works with students who come from nearby colleges to serve as volunteers with Lifewerks, Inc.'s Giving Garden food pantry. Lifewerks is a 501c3 nonprofit started by Joy and her husband, Chuck Kieffer, to mentor students of various ages. In the course of mentoring, they discovered that food comes before learning. It's very hard to concentrate when you're hungry.

Money raised by the sale of this and other student planners will help Joy as she enlarges the Lifewerks Giving Garden student food programs as well as other Lifewerks programs using college students to mentor younger students.

Want to Learn More? ~ Want to be Inspired?

Joy offers inspirational posts and quirkiness on her website at **joykieffer.com**. Sign up for the newsletter to get freebies such as extra journal pages, timely garden tips, book chapters from upcoming books, and activity pages.

**If you like this journal, and you'd like to help the author and the nonprofit she runs, please consider giving a review where you purchased this book. Verified purchase reviews improve the chance that others will discover this book. Positive reviews are gold!

~ ~ ~ Other Books by Joy Kieffer ~ ~ ~

It's only one small semester

The same book as the one in your hand, except it's smaller ~ for those who prefer a size that won't be confused with a text book. 7.5 x 9.25"

The UnRipe Gardener's Journal, Planner & Log Book

For the passionate gardener, the original journal is ideal and the reviews are stellar. However, some who consider themselves "average gardeners" say the original journal
has too many forms. They simply don't have time or the experience to take advantage of all it has to offer.

This version makes record-keeping simple, without losing vital information. The individual plant pages are check-box easy, and give instant info on each plant.

Includes logs for weather, bloom and harvest times, cultivation and propagation, disease and pest treatment, soil testing and amendments, and formulas, a zone map, graph pages coupled with lined pages for your garden bed layouts, a diary section, and individual plant
pages.

The Garden Journal, Planner & Log Book

The original and most in-depth garden journal of the series, designed for the knowledgable and passionate gardener.

The Garden Diary, Journal & Log Book

The simplest journal in the series, for those who want a place to keep minimal records. This journal has the same garden bed graphs and accompanying lined pages, diary pages, zone map, weights and measure conversion tables as the journal you hold in your hand. Nothing more.